THREADS
OF
HOPE

—◦—

An Offering for
Those Who Grieve

by
Beth Rotondo

STILLPOINT PRESS
Weymouth, Massachusetts

THREADS OF HOPE
An Offering for Those Who Grieve
by Beth Rotondo

Published by Stillpoint Press
157 Mt. Vernon Rd. East
Weymouth, MA 02189

© 2004 Beth Rotondo
All rights reserved
No part of this book may be used or reproduced in any manner
without the prior written permission from the author except for
brief quotations embodied in critical articles and reviews.

Cover and book design, typography & composition by
Arrow Graphics, Inc., Watertown, Massachusetts
Printed in the United States of America

ISBN: 0-9760165-0-8
Library of Congress Control Number:
2004095809

Third Printing 2008

Acknowledgments

It is the love of many people that brings me to this place in my life. I cannot name them all but know you are all treasured as significant in my life.

To all the people that I have sat with and listened to your stories of loss, I am grateful. You are the teachers of what it is like to walk in darkness.

To those who have guided me with patience and wisdom, through the process of writing and publishing this book , I thank you.

To my mom…You are generous and loving and know in your own soul the meaning of grief and the joy of life. Your beacon shines bright.

To my family…Your support and love have enabled me to continue to believe in myself.

To my friends…who love me from choice…your consistent and steadfast presence has encouraged me to reach for the unknown.

To my sons…you make me proud to call you my own.

To my husband…in whom I rest in complete safety and love…to you I call …home.

Contents

Introduction / vii

One
How long will this last? / 1

Two
Will I ever stop hurting? / 9

Three
What does moving on mean? / 19

Four
When should I change their things? / 25

Five
Am I going crazy? / 33

Six
Why should I go on? / 41

Seven
Why, Why, Why? / *49*

Eight
Who am I now? / *57*

Nine
Will I be happy again? / *65*

Ten
Why do I feel so guilty? / *73*

Eleven
Why don't they understand? / *81*

Twelve
How do I make a life for myself? / *89*

Afterward / *98*

Introduction

———◆———

Like the circles of water emanating from the drop of a stone, grief flows to the outer and inner shores of our lives. Its steady ripples find hidden nooks. It takes on a rhythm all its own.

When we experience the loss of a loved one through death, we find ourselves in a rhythm of life we have seldom encountered before. We are thrown into a world of the unknown. Only if we were dying ourselves would we walk this path. And because of the unknown, all kinds of emotions as well as experiences enter our lives uninvited. What we do with these unexpected "guests" will determine whether we integrate this painful time into our lives or hold it at bay.

This is a book of questions. Why questions? They echo down the long hallways of darkness during our grieving time. I am not writing this book to answer these questions. Profound change in our lives deserves exploration. We need time to get our bearings. I hope it will be a forum to discuss them, reword them and come to some understanding within ourselves regarding their meaning in our own lives.

There will be many questions we will ask ourselves while we grieve. Some of the questions have simple answers. But other questions invite us to go deeper than the "how to" answers. Sometimes we may hear ourselves give the same answers over and over again. Sometimes our answers will change. Sometimes we may hear silence. And sometimes we may experience a truth that only our heart knows. Read this book when you are struggling with these questions. My hope is that it will offer you reassurance and companionship on this journey of grief.

I have sat with many people through their grief and the thoughts that I share with you here are a result of the courage and resilience and faith of those people. I owe them much gratitude because working in the field of grief, working with the heart, keeps us honest about the journey of the heart.

In Remembrance

———◆———

my Son

my Dad

my Brother

It's so hard to know if I'm getting better. There are times when I feel like I can get up in the morning and carry on with a sense of normalcy. But there are those other times when I feel like I am in a downward spiral. I don't know if I'm getting better or getting worse.

One

HOW LONG WILL THIS LAST?

People hunger for an answer to this question. We think we can endure just about anything if we know there will be an end to it.

Those of us who have had children may remember what people told us while we were pregnant, "Don't worry about the pain in labor...you won't remember it after the baby is born." The pain of

*I can't stand feeling this way.
Just tell me when this will be over.
Then at least I know there will be
an end to this constant pain.*

labor ended when the baby was born. With grief, it doesn't work that way.

Grief work is not linear work. It is not like a cut or a broken limb that gets better with each passing day. That is a linear process. There are many symbols for grief. Let me share a few of them with you in order to understand the process of grief....

Grief is like a roller coaster, it always moves forward, but there are many dips and valleys....Grief is like a boat on the ocean. There are times when the waves gently rock the boat and then there are times when the force of the waves is so strong, the boat feels like it will topple....People feel like they are a boat

*Isn't there some kind of plan for this?
Can't you give me some magic pill
or wave a magic wand or something?*

THREADS OF HOPE

that has lost its compass or rudder. They are lost at sea, drifting, aimless, searching for direction....Grief is like a solar system. Death is the middle planet and we are in orbit around it. Sometimes we are searingly close to it and wonder if we will ever be released from its pull. Other times we are orbiting at a distance, viewing it from a different perspective.... Grief is beyond time. Sometimes it feels like yesterday, other times it feels like centuries ago.

At the beginning of our process, we are inside of grief. It encompasses everything we do or say. Everything takes on a greater significance. We see the world from the lens of grief. It overwhelms us and hits us behind the knees. As we con-

THREADS OF HOPE

tinue our process, grief becomes a part of us, inside of us. It begins to have a boundary, although it still comes into our day, uninvited.

We use symbols and images to describe an event, this death, because it is so beyond anything we have ever experienced. That is why poetry, music, the arts are so helpful when we are full of any emotion. They help us go beyond the limits of words in order to meet the limitlessness of our human emotion. They help our hearts speak.

How long will this last? Longer than we thought and longer than we want.

This can't possibly get better. I feel so devastated, so overwhelmed. How could I ever experience happiness again when I have lost the most important person in my life? Don't tell me that. I don't believe it.

THREADS OF HOPE

Two

WILL I EVER STOP HURTING?

Pain breaks open the shell of understanding. Grief brings feelings to us that are expected and unexpected. The obvious and more acceptable ones are sadness, loneliness, and feelings of being cheated. The less obvious are resentment, unresolved issues within the relationship, anger and fear. Grief becomes a blanket that covers every inch of our life. Nothing feels the

Sometimes the pain is so bad, so deep, so constant, I think I'm going to die from it. Why is this happening to me? I can't believe this is my life now… no happiness, no future.

THREADS OF HOPE

same anymore. Nothing looks the same. Nothing is the same. Our world, as we once knew it, has stopped. Nothing feels important and not much has meaning in our lives. As time goes on, we feel more isolated because our family and friends have continued with the routine of their lives but our routines have stopped with the sudden force of an earthquake. Our whole world is shaking…nothing feels anchored or sure. We wait for death to strike again, like a dark stranger lurking behind every corner.

Many things determine our reaction to our loss. In our culture, there seems to be a judgment on loss. A child's death is determined to be a greater loss than a sibling's death; a tragic death by accident

THREADS OF HOPE

receives more sympathy than a suicide or drug overdose. A sudden death will cause a different reaction than one that involved a long illness. A young spouse may feel differently than an older spouse. Your personal history with the person who died will also factor into your grief response as well as your personal history in response to any death.

Grief work is heart work. We have been wounded in ways we are not even aware of. As time goes on we feel the implication of our loss. It sears into our lives like a rope burn. We find ourselves wanting our old life back. We want to feel carefree and unencumbered. Every decision feels monumental. We feel

THREADS OF HOPE

lonely. We yearn for the past—for comfort and safety.

Our pain will lessen and ease when we begin to accept the present as the present. We cannot have the past back. Death is the immovable event in our lives. It is unyielding. We cannot move it or change it. We sometimes feel like Rumpelstilskin, stamping our feet, wanting our lives the way we once knew them, even though they were not perfect. We know in our heads that our loved ones are not coming back and yet our hearts yearn for their return. We remember and need to remember. We need to touch the fabric of our history so we can weave it into our present life. We are creating a tapestry.

THREADS OF HOPE

And as we weave our history into this tapestry, we are unifying our head and our heart. Our pain softens, and we can finally take a breath.

I lost her sooner than I ever imagined. She was young, vibrant, eager for life and all it's rewards. I struggle every minute, every day. Maybe I could capture her spirit somehow, like a still photograph. Then, maybe, I

Three

WHAT DOES MOVING ON MEAN?

"You have to get on with your life." That phrase is said over and over again to people who are grieving. It is said with the best intention, not wanting that person to be in pain anymore. People don't want their loved ones to live in the past. They may say, "Keep busy". "Don't think about it so much. Concentrate on something else. Don't make it harder on yourself."

wouldn't feel like I was abandoning her whenever I did something without her.

People who are grieving may hear these phrases as hurtful, telling them to forget the person that they loved. "You can't live in the past," they may say. This is true. Our goal is to live in the present. But we take our past with us and we take our loved one with us also. Our past contributes and shapes us into who we are today.

Grief catapults us into the past. We linger and long for a familiar pattern in our daily routines. We try to imitate our loved one's habits, the way they thought, and what they would do in certain situations. We try to get a sense of who we are now without them. And all this takes time.

THREADS OF HOPE

As ironic as this may sound, we are moving on when we are doing our grief work. This is the task at hand…to weave the past into our present life. We will not be able to do that until we make peace with the most transforming event in our lives.

Moving on doesn't mean forgetting the past. It means taking the past with us with gratitude and allowing life to enter our lives again, moment by moment, day by day.

I came week after week. My grief was deep and untouchable. I had cared for my husband for ten years. I also worked outside my home, trying to keep a sense of myself in the midst of losing my married life, as I once knew it. But when my husband died, my world

Four

WHEN SHOULD I CHANGE THEIR THINGS?

Change is one of the most difficult things for us to deal with. We like things to remain the same. We want things to look the same; we want people to act the same. When things and people are predictable we feel everything is ok. We are in control and we feel safe. When we experience a death, nothing is the same. We are bombarded with so many changes from the inside as well as the *did fall apart. Many of my friends and family suggested ways to ease the pain. But nothing rang true to me. I felt alone and yet the bond with my husband was impenetrable. I did not change a thing in our house. My husband's bathrobe hung on the hook and the slippers stayed*

outside. Our feelings change from day to day, moment to moment. We cannot predict what the next hour will feel like, let alone the next day or week. We are moving so fast and yet at times, we are as stuck as slow moving molasses. We want to feel like we did yesterday. We want our world to look like it did yesterday. We want yesterday.

This is what mourning is all about …wanting the person we love to be back in our lives as we once knew them, touched them, talked to them, loved them. We find it difficult to change anything in our lives because with each change, we acknowledge that something profound has happened to us. Our definition of our lives, of who we are now,

under them, almost like they were waiting to be filled once again. His drawer was untouched…the watch, the wallet, tie clip, dimes, quarters…all his. Now they sit there, unattached, just as I sit, separated, searching for purpose and meaning in my life.

has altered in ways that seep into the center of our very being.

With each change we make, we accept our altered life: every time we struggle to say "I" rather than "we", change the way we go food shopping, learn about finances and forms, fumble with the laundry, decide what to do with the tools. We decide and decide a hundred different times how our lives will look now. We are moving from passive to active, from victim to being more in charge of our lives.

Most of us change very slowly. We go through the motions of change. And sometimes we need to do that…fake it till we make it. But change, profound

THREADS OF HOPE

change, comes from within us. And our world around us reflects that change.

So it may not be important when we change our loved one's things. It may be more important to transform ourselves from within, reflecting the profound change in our lives. With each movement, we continue to weave our tapestry. Like nature itself, we are changing from a person in waiting to a person who adapts to all the seasons of life.

The garage door opened. I heard the sound from the kitchen. Oh my god, he's home. And just as quickly, realized it was my daughter who was driving, not my husband who died eight months earlier.

THREADS OF HOPE

Five

AM I GOING CRAZY?

All is not lost when we lose someone we love. But it feels that way. Our world is turned upside down. Everything we thought was "for sure" is no longer valid. We may question who we are now, who are our friends now, what do we believe in now, where do we belong now. What sense does this make in our life and in the grand scheme of the universe? We may catapult from

It's 2:00. I should call her. I start to pick up the phone, a ritual I practiced for many years. I want to tell her something that happened at work. As I pick up the receiver, a thunderbolt crashes in my head. I quietly put the phone down. No one is there

questioning everything we ever knew as true, to not caring about anything or anyone. We do not know what a good night sleep means anymore. We are lucky if two or three hours of sleep gives us some peace. Our appetite has almost disappeared and our desire to cook has just as quickly vanished. We cannot keep our mind focused on anything. The pile of newspapers keeps getting higher because we just don't have the interest or focus to read them. We find ourselves not able to read even our favorite books. We may go from room to room, not remembering why we are there. And we may even stop in midsentence, not knowing what we are trying to say.

at the other end, waiting for my call.
I am alone, wondering if people see
me as exposed as I feel.

We think we are going crazy! We have never acted this way before, felt this way before, or thought this way before. It is very unnerving and very frightening. We hesitate to tell someone because we feel so vulnerable and unsure of ourselves.

You are not going crazy. These feelings and thoughts are very normal in grief. What you once thought was normal is no longer normal. Going through this difficult time is hard enough; but to think you may be doing or feeling something that is not acceptable makes it even more difficult and isolating. Therefore it is often helpful to talk to someone who understands the grieving process.

THREADS OF HOPE

It is very important to be patient with ourselves. When we are hurt, we want to protect our heart. We do not want to be wounded again. We do not willingly or eagerly open up or trust life anymore. We are like parched earth, unable to absorb any life-giving nourishment.

But given time and the warmth of love and acceptance, our frozen heart begins to thaw, soaking up the necessary ingredients for our sustenance and growth.

I question everything. My mind devours books and essays on pain and suffering. I doubt my religion, my relationship to my family and friends. I severed all ties to things my wife and I shared and enjoyed…our summer home, our favorite restaurants, and our social friends.

Six

WHY SHOULD I
GO ON?

This question has been asked hundreds of times in songs and in the quiet of the dark by people who are grieving. It is an existential question because it goes to the heart of our existence…why should we go on?

The purpose, the role, the reason we get up in the morning, may be gone. Nothing makes sense now. Everything we thought was safe and secure is tossed

I abandoned my heart and anything or anyone who gave me love and joy. I dutifully sit with my wife at her grave, talking with her, imploring her, unable to allow my heart to feel the loss of love and meaning in my life.

in the air. Our belief in the way the world should work, our religious beliefs are all shaken. We feel unanchored, not connected to anyone or anything. It is a very painful time but also an important time.

Our lives have meaning when our world is bigger than ourselves. For many, their spouse and family give them purpose. For some, it is their work. When grief strikes our world, we flounder in our beliefs. We may discover that we don't know what we believe. What context do we put this death into? How do we make sense of all of this?

These are difficult questions but necessary ones. We can eventually get to the point where we may stop crying and

THREADS OF HOPE

maybe even laugh. But in order for us to feel alive again, we have to figure out why we are getting up in the morning and what gives our life purpose and meaning. We can go through the motions of living but we will feel empty and unsatisfied.

These questions don't have quick and easy answers; and many people give quick and easy advice. These questions become the path for our journey in grief. Not all people go on this journey. Many just want the pain to go away. These questions are the essential threads in our tapestry, giving it a framework that will uphold all the stitching and various patterns in our lives.

THREADS OF HOPE

There are many sources for discovering and discussing how we accomplish this: the many forms of spiritual belief; the worlds of art, music, and nature; the quietness of our heart and soul.

Trust your heart. Trust this grief work. Your heart knows its true home.

You are not alone.

I just don't understand this. My wife was a good person. She would do anything for anyone. She was a good wife and a wonderful mother. Why is she gone and these other people, the people who do awful things to others, why are they still alive?

THREADS OF HOPE

Seven

WHY, WHY, WHY?

These three words echo in the darkness and vastness of the universe. What is the purpose of this question? What benefit will the answer give us? What reason will be good enough to satisfy our disbelief and outrage over what has happened to us?

It seems that by the very nature of the question, life has to defend itself. We have an idea as to how life should hap-

They say that God has a plan for us all. Well, I had some plans myself. What am I supposed to do now? None of this makes sense. Where do I go for some answers? Who has the answers? And what answer would ever make any sense to me?

pen, or at least how our life should happen. We grow up with a set of beliefs or expectations that we are either taught, or that we have somehow inculcated into our belief system. We all remember in our younger years, grade school perhaps, saying to our parents or teachers, that this or that was not fair. We were convinced that someone was being cruel or ignorant or both. If they knew better, they wouldn't be doing this to us.

We plead our case to no avail. We are answered in words that seemed so insensitive and uncaring. Life is not fair. Well, so what. Make it fair.

When a tragedy occurs in our life, it shakes the foundations of our belief

THREADS OF HOPE

system. Or it exposes the fact that we may not have any framework in which to fall back on and gain some understanding. We may come to realize that we believe only "bad" people should die earlier than their time and "good" people should be able to live their lives fully and uninterrupted. In grief, we struggle with everything. All that was solid and sure now seems frivolous or lacks meaning. Every decision we make feels like a huge decision. And yet the question that haunts us, that overshadows everything, is "why did this happen?"

One of the illusions we grow up believing in is that we are in control of our lives. If we are good, we will be rewarded. If we work hard, we will be

THREADS OF HOPE

promoted. If we love deeply enough, no one will leave us or die. Death makes us painfully aware that we are not in control of life. We may make decisions about our lives but we are not in control of life.

So the question to ask may be, what are we going to do now or how will we respond to what has happened to us? This we can control. We can become bitter and not trust, or we can wrestle with what life has given us and gain insight into ourselves.

We are mere players on the stage of life. The question is—how will we play our part?

I always saw myself as a competent person. I was wife and mother who raised two children and an administrator in the business community. I was organized and efficient, supervised with good communication skills, and had a plan of action for the success of my

Eight

WHO AM I NOW?

We feel like strangers to ourselves. We don't know who we are. We are feeling emotions we have never felt before...and some of these emotions we don't like. They make us feel uncomfortable, not like ourselves and out of control. They are so powerful they scare us. We thought we knew who we were and yet we are nothing like we used to be. We feel changed, altered, *business. When my husband died, my world and my sense of myself changed suddenly and dramatically. I felt out of control. I couldn't decide what to wear, let alone what the agenda would be at the board meeting. I thought I was the independent one. Now I realize how* adrift. We thought we had a sense of order about how our life was going and now everything has changed.

One of the ways we define ourselves is in relationship to others. We have defined roles and ways of being. We are wife, husband, mother, father, friend, brother, sister, co-worker, and the many other roles in our lives. We may have seen ourselves as dependent or self reliant, as self-assured or insecure, as quiet or outgoing. We rely on our partner to complete or compliment our inadequacies or insecurities.

When someone we love dies, we feel adrift, without purpose or maybe even hope of finding our sure footing again.

dependent I was on his quiet support, his humor and his love. I can barely get through the day without crying and I never think of the future without a fear that sends chills through my being. I wonder what to call myself. Am I still a wife? I still feel married. I hate that

We may find ourselves grasping for quick fixes such as drinking, drugs, eating, shopping and relationships. And we still feel alone, and unanchored.

We need to get to know ourselves again. One of the most difficult aspects of grief is patience. As the flower from the seed, we cannot hurry growth. We need to make friends with ourselves, allowing our feelings to be heard. Our fear is that we will be overtaken by these feelings and become a weak and incompetent person. It is only when we acknowledge these feelings that we can remove the power and fear of them.

We may discover and develop new aspects of ourselves. And we may even

word "widow". And I am definitely not single.

find that we feel more confident as time goes on and accomplishments increase. We begin to see ourselves differently. We see life differently. We begin to accept change. We learn to grow.

People tell me all the time…"You'll meet someone new. You're young, your whole life is in front of you." I feel my whole life is behind me…and it was the best part of my life.

THREADS OF HOPE

Nine

WILL I BE HAPPY AGAIN?

If the answer to this question were "yes", you would not believe me. The pain in grief can be so severe; we believe it will never cease. If the answer to the question is "no", then we relinquish the possibility of ever being happy again. We may think we will never be happy again, but we may still want someone to hold out hope for us. As Emily Dickenson wrote, "Hope is the

My friends tell me that this doesn't get any better. As time goes on, it just gets worse. How could this possibly get worse? I feel like a robot, just going through the motions of living. I'll never feel happy again. And I really don't care.

thing with feathers—that perches in the soul—And sings the tune without the words. And never stops at all."

In grief, we are tossed around like a leaf in the wind. Our feelings change so quickly we can't keep up with them. And neither can anyone else. In early grief, we don't really care about being happy. We just want to survive, sometimes. Our focus is wanting our old life back. We long for familiar patterns and feelings. But nothing is familiar. We wail and resist this change. We want our old life back. We want our loved one back. Our wound is deep and raw.

As with any wound, we need to take care of it and pay attention to it. Our

THREADS OF HOPE

pain is caused by our inability to accept this severe change in our life. Our healing depends on our ability to accept this change. This does not come easy. It can be unforeseen and unwelcome. Some of us kick and scream at every little change in our lives and others take life more in stride. But eventually all of us will come to a point in our process of grief where we will decide what we want out of our life now. Is it over? Or what do I want for myself now? This point becomes a fulcrum...a leverage point, a position, a life sentence for our entire life. Will we continue to look backward or will we risk our safety net to look forward? It is not important when we reach our fulcrum. It is important that we reach it.

THREADS OF HOPE

Being happy again is not disrespectful to our loved one. Being happy again is not abandoning our loved one. Being happy again means we have accepted the fact that we are alive. Being happy again means that it is ok for us to be alive. Being happy again means we have decided to live life, for that is the legacy of death.

I was sitting at the kitchen table yesterday, thinking of how my life has changed since death entered it so unexpectedly. I thought of how happy we were, how many wonderful things we did together, how fulfilled we were as a family. Then I started to think of all

Ten

WHY DO I FEEL SO GUILTY?

It is a haunting question. It hides behind smiles and appears in the quiet of the night. Could I have done something? Should I have done something? Whether the death was sudden or from an illness, we wonder. Was I not observant enough? Did I not notice they were sick? Should I have pushed them to see a doctor? Maybe I should have cooked healthier meals. We

the things I said I was going to do for you and didn't; of all the things I said to you that weren't exactly supportive and loving; of all the times I could have said "I love you" and didn't. I feel I let you down.

wonder. What could I have done to prevent this death? Or maybe we even say, we should have prevented this death.

Guilt is not simple or straightforward. It usually sneaks up on us and blindsides us. It may shadow our life and color it unworthy. We are not perfect human beings and consequently our relationships are not perfect. When we look back at our lives, we may see things we said or didn't say, things we did or didn't do and feel like we really messed up…we came up short. We may say we should have died, not them. We feel unworthy. We believe that somehow and in some illogical way, we could have prevented this death if we did things differently or said things differently.

THREADS OF HOPE

Death is the immovable event in our lives. We try to negotiate it and nothing works. We try to recreate our past and that doesn't change anything either. We try to change ourselves and that doesn't bring them back. We face the inevitable fact that we are helpless in stopping death. And we don't like it.

We then slowly come to the realization that our loved one has died and is not coming back. We may be surprised how long this takes. But once we realize that, something else occurs to us. We are alive. We may not feel alive. Most of the time, we are barely surviving. But with the acknowledgement that we are alive, we may feel guilt. And with guilt as our partner, we sabotage our ability to nur-

THREADS OF HOPE

ture ourselves. We feel it's wrong to be happy. We feel it's wrong to enjoy the warmth of the sun or the smile of a friend. Our loved one would not think it is wrong. But guilt is a cruel companion.

We need to choose who will walk with us: guilt, with all it's stinginess and depletion, or love, with its power to nurture and embrace life.

"You're so different now. Where is the old "you"? Don't dwell on it so much." I hear these and countless other directives many times from many people. They either tell me to keep busy or they avoid bringing his name into the conversation…like he never existed.

Eleven

WHY DON'T THEY UNDERSTAND?

We thought they'd be there for us. We thought we wouldn't have to say much and they would knowingly acknowledge our pain. We thought we wouldn't have to ask for understanding and patience. We thought it would flow freely from our history with them and from the ties of family. We thought we would only miss our loved one and

I am hurt and confused, feeling the loss of support from my family and friends. But I am also beginning to doubt myself. It's been six months. Maybe I should be "over" it by now. Some people avoid me like the plague. Maybe it's me.

now we find ourselves missing our support system.

We expected when people said "call me if you need anything," that they would be there when we called. We expected that when someone said, "I understand" that they really did know the depth and breadth of our pain.

We are discovering that the journey of grief is a solitary one and one not easily understood unless one has traveled that friendless road.

When someone dies, people have various reactions to the person who grieves. They may feel compassion for the surviving spouse or bereft parent. But they may also feel fear. They have

THREADS OF HOPE

been brushed with mortality. They have glimpsed an unimaginable pain that they feel is best kept at bay. And they may feel the best way to deal with this possibility of death is to avoid it and you. So they may not ask you how you are because you might answer them truthfully. They might feel your pain. They might imagine their loved one gone and cannot tolerate it. And they may not know how to comfort you when they have not bridged the chasm of life's experience by focusing on you and not on their own fear.

This journey of grief is not easily embraced. People may appear callous, and some may be. But many just cannot imagine a pain so deep, so constant and so encompassing. Most of us would

THREADS OF HOPE

rather retreat to the illusions we live with rather than live with the unknown.

And that is what death teaches us. It leads us down roads we never would have discovered or chosen. We meet people we once thought of as strangers but now are fellow travelers in this new world.

People do not understand because not many choose to walk the path with us. So it comes back to us. This is our journey. This is our task at hand. We would love a buddy on this trip but it is solely our path. We may invite people to come. But don't slow down to defend or explain. Walk on, walk on. There will be gifts along the way.

How do I possibly start a new life for myself? I feel overwhelmed. I never liked the bar scene. I was married to the most loving person in the world. How could I possible be lucky twice?

Twelve

HOW DO I MAKE A LIFE FOR MYSELF?

Did you ever plant a garden or build something from scratch? Or even bake or cook something, not prepared or ready-made, not frozen and prepackaged, but with your own ideas, plans, ingredients and work? Well, that is how we make a life for ourselves.

We wonder, where do I begin? We begin by having an idea. What do we want our lives to look like? We really

I feel my loss has taken over my life. I think about it everyday. Sometimes I feel I am drowning in it. Where is the door that leads out? And what is behind that open door. Sometimes that scares me more than anything else.

have to believe in ourselves. We need to believe that we are worthy of having a life by ourselves and for ourselves. In the garden, we decide where our garden will be placed, how big or small it will be. Do we want a blazing sun garden, shaded garden or maybe a dappled one? Just like the garden, we decide what our lives will look like. Stimulating with lots of activities; quiet and contemplative or a little bit of both.

Next comes the plan. How do we do this? We have to decide what kind of plants will thrive in the location of our garden. For sunny gardens, we buy the flowers or plants that can withstand the heat. With dappled or shady gardens, our plants will be different. With our lives,

THREADS OF HOPE

we decide what kind of activities we enjoy. What are our interests? What kind of people? Do we like quiet places or high-energy ones? What will satisfy and fulfill our inner most selves.

Now we pick out the ingredients. In the garden, we need hardy plants that will withstand what nature offers on an everyday basis. When we cook, the quality of the meal depends on the quality of the ingredients we choose. So to in our lives. If we surround ourselves with mediocre or unsatisfying activities, and even toxic and negative people, we will be unhappy. We need to choose ingredients that will enable our spirit to soar and thrive.

THREADS OF HOPE

We nourish our garden in many different ways. We prepare soil that will feed our plants. We may use compost, rich soil with remnants of the past. We also need to water our garden. Our earth will become parched and barren without sufficient food. We need to pay attention because every day the garden is changing. There could be some pests taking over. And we need patience. Did you notice that anything that grows, takes time. Not much grows over night.

In our desire to build a life for ourselves, remember the lessons nature offers us. We work hard building a life for ourselves. We may wish someone could do it for us and/or with us. But to be truly happy, we need to plant the seed;

THREADS OF HOPE

we need to water this precious seed; we need to protect it from the harsh forces of nature; and we will smile when after patience, hard work and time, we begin to feel our feet are on the ground. We begin to see the roots of our new life taking hold.

Afterward

We will experience many milestones in our journey of grief. We will learn much. We will endure more than we ever thought possible. We will continue to learn how to live moment-to-moment, day-to-day. We are weaving the richness of the past into our tapestry. Its color is burnt gold, singed with our pain but beautiful within the other colors and seasons of our life. We will be less afraid. We will be stronger.

But we have also experienced the rhythm of this grief work. We now know we will have dark days as well as good days, maybe even weeks. We now know our sense of well-being will vanish as quickly or silently as it came. We may be discouraged and even feel exhausted.

Return to this book for reassurance and comfort. Return to this book when you question, struggle, and go deeper, living with uncertainty. For it is in this uncertainty, this unknown, that we allow truth, love, and understanding to enter our hearts in new ways.

Somewhere during our process of grief, we will slowly move from mourning for our loved one to accepting the fact that they abide within us. We will see life differently and we will be grateful. That is what death teaches….